SECRETS

The Conflicted Role of First-Generation Nigerian American Women Experiencing Domestic Violence

Dr. Umo Ntekim

SECRETS
THE CONFLICTED ROLE OF FIRST-GENERATION NIGERIAN AMERICAN WOMEN EXPERIENCING DOMESTIC VIOLENCE

iUniverse books may be ordered through booksellers or by contacting:

iUniverse
1663 Liberty Drive
Bloomington, IN 47403
www.iuniverse.com
844-349-9409

Because of the dynamic nature of the Internet, any web addresses or links contained in this book may have changed since publication and may no longer be valid. The views expressed in this work are solely those of the author and do not necessarily reflect the views of the publisher, and the publisher hereby disclaims any responsibility for them.

Any people depicted in stock imagery provided by Getty Images are models, and such images are being used for illustrative purposes only.
Certain stock imagery © Getty Images.

ISBN: 978-1-6632-2914-4 (sc)
ISBN: 978-1-6632-2915-1 (e)

Print information available on the last page.

iUniverse rev. date: 10/21/2021

PREFACE

The Conflicting Role of First-Generation Nigerian Women Living in Southern California Who Experienced Domestic Violence as a Result of Acculturation.

The purpose of the study was to examine the conflicting role of first-generation Nigerian women living in Southern California who experienced domestic violence as a result of acculturation. The goal of this study was to identify the views of these women and to build upon the scope of research-based literature that may improve the plight of these women who self-identify as victims of domestic violence. I addressed the issue of conflicting roles by examining the relationship among acculturation and domestic violence in twenty first-generation Nigerian women divorced or married to Nigerian men in Southern California.

These key research questions were asked:

a. What is the role of cultural factors contributing to abuse?
b. What systemic factors contribute to abuse?
c. What factors affect women's ability to seek help and services?

The primary method employed in this research study was in-depth interviews guided by a qualitative research framework. Twenty Nigerian women were interviewed. Fifteen of these women reported that culture is a factor contributing to domestic violence. The systemic factors that contributed to abuse included abuse, anger, fear, lack of support, and financial problems. When thirteen of the women were asked, "What factor affects women's ability to seek help and services?" the top responses were fear, work-life balance, and argumentative.

ACKNOWLEDGMENTS

I would like to acknowledge and give thanks to my children, all family members and friends for their love and support.

I dedicate this book to my late father and mother, Mr. and Mrs. William Bassey; my late sisters, Mary and Eno and my family.

CONTENTS

TABLES

CHAPTER 1

Introduction

The prevalence and influence of domestic abuse of Nigerian women living in Southern California is creating fear, anxiety, and loss of hope among these middle-class women. In Nigeria, women are not expected to pay bills and taxes; all family expenses are incurred by men. Most of the Nigerian women coming to the United States had high hopes for a more successful life than they had back home. Most Nigerian women in the United States are expected to work and earn a reasonable income, but some have been disappointed by low-paying jobs with meager salaries. In contrast, some of the men are unwilling to change the standards to which they are accustomed, preventing their wives from working, forcing the women to remain perpetual housewives under their tight control. These men become abusive while working more than one job to provide for the entire family. This new way of life forces these women to be submissive to their abusive husbands to the point that they will not even report abuse to the authorities because of fear of being punished by their abusive partners (Nworah, 2010). This type of environment helps to promote domestic abuse and suppresses these women's ability to live like their host counterparts. For some of these women, in addition to fear of abuse, several fears—of deportation, financial hardship, being blamed for their husband's arrest, and shame and harassment by friends and extended family—prevent the abused women from getting good-paying jobs; they therefore rely solely on their abusive husbands to provide for them. This situation lends itself to dependency and unnecessary control, the byproducts of domestic violence (Hardy et al., 2012).

Moreover, unemployment, lack of social support and institutional discrimination create barriers for some of these women, hampering the women's ability to progress professionally and consequently affecting their domestic lives, which eventually results in an increased tendency toward domestic violence (Anitha, 2008).

Problem Statement

Even though there are no current statistics on the problem of domestic violence in Nigerian Women in Southern California, a comparison study conducted in Canada among Nigerian women immigrants reveals that 29 % of married women have been abused by their partners at least once (Statistics Canada, 2002). Within the Nigerian communities in Southern California, cultural differences play significant roles in the level and intensity of domestic violence. There is an increase in the prevalence of this problem because of the married Nigerian men's mind-set of male supremacy or dominance over women in the typical Nigerian culture. Moreover, according to Nworah (2010), there is also an apparent cultural clash among married Nigerian women, who are trying to adjust their attitudes toward their husbands based on the prevailing norms as immigrants. Because the current intervention methodologies and domestic abuse-prevention methods no longer seem to be working in these communities, an urgent need for close attention to these problems therefore exists.

Background and Significance of the Problem

According to the World Health Organization (WHO, 1999) and Liebmann (2012), ethnicity is an important proxy of cultural factors affecting domestic violence, as encompasses values and norms that govern the behavioral and psychological levels of women's participation in decision making and power relations within households and at community levels. Ethnicity may also reflect openness to the influences and/or adherence to other cultures due to interactions from different areas and/or regions. Culture can also affect domestic violence indirectly through education and modernization. According to the WHO (1999), there have been reports of risks many women face around the world. One in four women had experienced violence, which includes physical and sexual abuse, by their husbands and partners in their lifetime. Evidence suggests that more than half of these cases are accompanied by sexual violence and nonconsensual sexual relationship, resulting in life- threating reproductive problems such as unplanned pregnancy (WHO, 1999).

It was hypothesized by Agnew (1998) and Mann and Takyi (2009) that the higher the age of respondents, the greater the likelihood that their view of patriarchy would affect their responses to the issue of wife abuse, especially domestic violence. That is, older women are more likely to give a positive response or support that a woman should be beaten under some circumstances than are younger ones. In their studies, age was sub grouped into three categories in a bivariate analysis and measured as continuous at the multivariate level.

Religion is believed to have a profound impact on individual behavior and views. Even in the face of modernization and its con- sequences on cultural practices, religion seems to hold a firm grip on moral values relating to power relations between wife and husband. Women who are more religious are therefore more likely to hold strong, rigid, and fundamentalist types of beliefs that may encourage abuse; however, the relationship between religious affiliation and domestic violence, particularly wife beating, is likely to be mediated by social and demographic factors such as education of the respondent. Basically, all religions—Christianity, Islam, and others—expect the woman to be submissive and the man to be the head of the household (Brownridge, 2002). Some researchers, such as Hindin and Adair (2002) and Oropesa (1997), have found male control of household decision making to be a good predictor of domestic violence. My study examined men's attitudes toward women making economic decisions in the household.

With more than 389 ethnic groups in Nigeria, ethnic differences are critical in explaining cultural differences, interpersonal relationships, communication, and conflict-resolution mechanisms. The heterogeneity of ethnic groups in Nigeria implies that social change takes place at different paces and nonuniformly. Ethnic groups in the WHO (1999) study were regrouped into six categories: Hausa/Fulani, Igbo, Yoruba, northern minorities, southern minorities, and others (which include nationals of other countries). The WHO found that ethnic affiliation serves as a proxy for culture. Thus, many social and economic factors create barriers for the immigrant woman who is battered. Leaving her husband for a safer environment may mean losing not only his financial support and her possessions but also the extended family or community that can provide her with the support needed to obtain work (Erez, 2000).

Studies by Agnew (1998) have indicated that education is negatively related to domestic violence. Educated women are more likely to interact with people of varied experiences than those who are not educated; they were therefore expected to be less supportive of and to have negative attitudes or views about wife beating. Because female education appears to be the most influential factor affecting attitudes about wife beating, it is therefore relevant for researchers and clinicians to understand how female education level interacts with other covariates and its effects on women's perception of domestic violence. In view of the paucity of research on regional differential in family violence, I found it imperative in my research to explore the phenomenon with data from the Nigeria Demographic and Health Survey (2003), which contains comparable and representative regional information. Educational categories used include nonschooled, as well as primary, secondary, and postsecondary education, representing the respondents' highest level of education attained.

Apart from identifying the structural patterns within the Nigerian community, the issue of region is appropriate in helping us understand socioeconomic and cultural influences on respondents' views of domestic violence. It is also important that regions constitute a proxy of social change or development. There may be a higher prevalence of abuse in the Niger Delta region of Nigeria because of tribal belief differences. For example, the Akwa Ibom family dynamics are different from the Imo and Yoruba state family dynamics. Nigeria comprises thirty-six states that are organized into six geopolitical zones. The Niger Delta region includes states from different geopolitical zones, and the states of Abia and Imo (known as Igbo), Akwa Ibom, and Cross Rivers (known as Ibibio); Bayelsa and River (known as Ijaw); Delta and Edo (Benin and Itsekiri); and Ondo (Yoruba) are fundamentally different from one another. The significantly different cultures of these ethnic groups govern the status of women and how women are treated, as culture is an important dimension of all societies, as it is a way of life that is transmitted from one generation to another.

Regardless of their status, women are vulnerable to a whole spectrum of preventable domestic violence (Martin et al., 2002). As a social phenomenon, culture governs how members of society behave and defines their roles and how they relate to one another, particularly between sexes and among age groups.

The traditional African culture confers superior status on males and subordinate status on females. Accordingly, males are brought up to understand that they are future heads of their house- holds; they must learn how to take charge, and they must know how to exercise power and authority in the household, which then becomes domestic violence. By contrast, females are brought up to learn how to understand and obey authority, as well as to believe that they always will be taken care of and protected—in other words, females should be seen and not heard. These practices signal the differential role expectations between males and females in their future marital relationships, in which domestic abuse increases.

Just as societies are not static, however, cultures and their associated practices change over time. Two important factors that contribute to changes in cultural practices are the levels of poverty and illiteracy in a society. Families that are economically well off embrace education and are well disposed to send both their male and female children to college. Unfortunately, in the Niger Delta region, where the levels of poverty and illiteracy are high, parents cannot afford to send their female children to college; consequently, uneducated married females generally tend to accept as a fait accompli the cultural subordinate role assigned to them. Even among educated women, however, societal sanctions could contribute to married women feeling forced to stay or continue in abusive relationships. Such societal sanctions can include fear of disownment by family, rejection by friends, and loneliness. The situation in the Niger Delta region of Nigeria has assumed a frightening dimension with social and economic implications; the rising insecurity resulting from the upsurge of violence and cult activities has affected the dignity and quality of women's lives in the region.

Domestic violence against women is a serious societal and major health problem with several adverse consequences (Nasir & Hyder, 2003; Neggers, Goldenberg, Cliver, & Hauth, 2004). The cultural disposition and stigma attached to violence seem to vitiate the basic human rights of women in the Niger Delta region, however, making it impossible for women to leave the violence or seek help. According to researchers Abasiubong, Abasiattai, Bassey, and Ogunsemi (2010), "It is important to be cognizant of the experiences of the women in the midst of these adversities" (p. 893). These researchers examined the frequency of occurrences and identified demographic risk factors of violence among pregnant women in Uyo, a community in the Niger Delta region of Nigeria. They hoped their findings would help healthcare providers and lawmakers become aware of the risk of violence and its adverse effects on mothers and children and to promote its prevention. The results of the study showed that violence among pregnant women is prevalent in Uyo, and, unfortunately, that domestic violence is ignored in most cases despite being a major health problem. Despite the fact that many of the abuses occur behind closed doors with no adequate information, the lifetime prevalence rate of 33.1 percent in the study is significant. In addition, the index rate of 22.9 percent among pregnant women shows that domestic violence is ongoing.

According to Abasiubong et al. (2010), although there has been increasing global concern about the level of violence against women, little has been done regarding domestic violence in the Nigerian community. There has been evidence from general observations that there may be a higher prevalence of domestic violence in the Niger Delta region of Nigeria. Even with the emerging and alarming social indicators for violence against women in the area, little effort has been made to address this dangerous trend.

To determine the factors associated with domestic violence, researchers Obi and Ozumba (2007) completed a study by a cross-sectional survey carried out at two tertiary health institutions in southeast Nigeria from January 2005 to March 2005. The study involved 600 men seen at the outpatient departments of the two hospitals during these months. The results showed more than 70 percent of respondents reported abuse in their family toward their wives. The study showed that the domestic violence was significantly associated with alcohol abuse, increased age disparity between couples, influential in-laws, and unemployment. According to the study, there was gross underreporting of domestic violence due to cultural factors, embarrassment, and repercussions that could follow such reports.

Even though there has not been a study specifically on domestic violence against Nigerian women living in Southern California, there have been incidents of Nigerian women in Southern California being killed by their husbands as a result of domestic violence. According to Ladepo (2014), there is an epidemic. In the article "An Epidemic: Nigerian Men Killing Their Nurse Wives in the US," he provides commentary about the rude awakening experienced by Nigerian men acculturating to the United States when they realize their nurse wives make more money than them, which leads to domestic violence.

Purpose of the Study

In studies conducted by researchers such as Abasiubong et al. (2010), Olawale (2010), and Beeman (2002), women's perception of domestic violence was measured based on their responses to questions about whether they agree that a husband is justified in hitting or beating his wife when she burns the food, argues with him, goes out without telling him, neglects the children, and refuses to have sex with him. The results revealed that roughly three- fifths (62.4 percent) of women agreed that a husband is justified for beating his wife for at least one of the mentioned circumstances. Half of the respondents agreed that a husband is correct in beating his wife if she goes out without telling him, and just under half (48.5 percent) agreed that she should be beaten if she neglects the children. A smaller percentage of the women supported wife beating if a woman argues with her husband (42.9 percent) or refuses to have sex with him (36.7 percent), and three out of ten women felt that a husband is right in beating his wife if she burns the food.

This evidence in the research literature regarding the perspectives of the Nigerian American middle-aged women living in United States and those older generations of women who came to the United States in the late 1970s is inadequate and unsubstantiated, according to Beeman (2002). The core of this book therefore explores this generational gap between the older and younger generations that migrated from Nigeria to America. I have studied the perceptions and views of these Nigerian American women in Southern California in hopes of improving the plight of women who self-identify as victims of intimate partner violence.

I addressed the issue of acculturation and assimilation by examining the relationships among acculturation, domestic violence, and mental health in five Nigerian women married to Nigerian men in Southern

California. I also examined whether domestic violence was initiated or exacerbated by resettlement stressors, such as language barriers and cultural differences (Darvishpour, 2002; Min, 2001).

Further, I examined the relationship between domestic abuse, its effect on the job market, and how it is affected by the job market—specifically how lower-level jobs, lower income, and unstable employment increase domestic violence. The study also addressed the fears of women who are unable to find stable and good employment because of having unauthorized immigration status (Liebmann, 2012).

CHAPTER 2

Literature Review

D omestic violence is described as "a pattern of abusive behaviour which escalates in frequency and severity over time" (Bartels, 2005, p. 1). According to this definition, domestic violence is not onetime abuse but abuse that repeats, establishing a pattern that spirals into extreme outcomes, such as severe physical injuries or even death. Laws protecting women and children from this crime have been ratified and implemented in many countries. A study by Kishor and Johnson (2005) reported, "Violence against women, committed by an intimate partner is an important public health and human rights issue. In recent years, attention has focused also on intimate partner violence during pregnancy due to its prevalence, adverse health consequences, and intervention potential" (p. 259). These authors discovered that women in countries in which men are the decision makers for the household, such as Cambodia, Colombia, the Dominican Republic, Egypt, Haiti, India, Nicaragua, Peru, and Zambia, experience domestic violence from their spouses regardless of the women's physical states. This implies that the women in these countries are abused even during pregnancy. Generally, the study indicates that such abuse is detrimental to the health and rights of women as well as to the development of the individual nations.

Perceptions of Domestic Violence

Studies on domestic violence in Nigeria have not examined perceptions, either qualitatively or quantitatively, of that abuse. In fact, only two available studies used qualitative tools to ask questions about such perceptions. These largely small qualitative studies concluded that domestic violence, especially wife battering, is perceived as an acceptable way of life. The explanation of the acceptance of wife beating is based on the existing power imbalances within the home and the society at large (Breitenbecher & Scarce, 1999). One such study conducted by Beeman (2002) among the Tiv-speaking people of the Benue State highlighted this perception with a profound statement from Odimegwu (2001), which was commonly expressed: "If you are not yet beaten by your husband, then you do not know the joy of marriage, and that means you are not yet married" (p. 17). The results from this study provide quantitative corroboration of this perception. Beeman measured women's perception of domestic violence based on their responses to questions about whether a husband is justified in hitting or beating his wife when she burns the food, argues with him, goes out without telling him, neglects the children, or refuses to have sex with him. Roughly 62.4 percent of the women agreed that a husband is justified for beating his wife in at least one of these circumstances. Additionally, half of the women agreed that a husband is correct in beating his wife if she goes out without telling him, and just under half agreed that she should be beaten if she neglects the children. A smaller percentage of the women supported wife beating if a woman argues with her husband (42.9 percent) or refuses to have sex with him (36.7 percent), and three out of ten women felt that a husband is right to beat his wife if she burns the food.

Immigration Process

Immigrant woman who have joined their husbands in other countries are often fearful of reporting their abusive husbands out of fear of being deported. While the immigration documentation is still pending, to be completed by the husband, the woman is afraid of reporting domestic abuse, and women who are of illegal immigration status have difficulties leaving abusive relationships or calling for help (Anitha, 2008).

Anitha's (2008) article examines the extent to which England's Labour government's policy toward immigrant women experiencing domestic violence responds to those women's needs. The research was conducted in 2007 by quantitative interviews of thirty south Asian women living in England and with no access to public funds or resources because of their recent marriage and/or immigration status. The Domestic Violence Rule was examined in light of the reality of south Asian women's experiences, including the nature of domestic violence they face, their patterns of help seeking, pathways out of the abusive relationships, and their experience of services provision (Immigration Rules, 2002). According to Anitha, "Before 2002, women who faced domestic violence during the probationary period had the tough 'choice' of either ending the violence because of their insecure immigration status or leaving the abusive relationship and returning to their country of origin, often to face further abuse from their own family for having ended the marriage, or staying here as an illegal immigrant" (p. 190). Other researchers, such as Yearnshire (1997) and Hester (2006), believed that most women experiencing domestic violence do not call the police due because of men's control over the women using threats of deportation.

Culture Shock

Both women and men who have immigrated to the United States sometimes experience feelings of estrangement, anger, frustration, loneliness, unhappiness, homesickness, and hostility. Women immigrants experience additional cultural shock in the first few years because of fear of seeking appropriate resources and having little or no support system. For example, finding health care and knowing where to purchase food and other daily needs can be intimidating (Mann & Takyi, 2009). During the state of disorientation that can come over anyone who is in unknown surroundings and out of one's comfort zone, as with immigrants, adjustment issues that can affect the individual's ability to secure employment generally include culture shock, health-related concerns, loss of status, and family dynamics (Drachman & Halberstadt, 1992). According to Margaretha (2002), cultural shock has been defined as "the anxiety caused from contact with a new culture combined with feelings of confusion, loss, and powerlessness that accompany the loss of familiar cultural cues and social norms."

Immigrants often experience cultural shock, which, because of the overwhelming strain of their experience, interferes with their ability to gather information, solve problems, and make decisions (Westwood & Ishiyama, 1991). "The degree to which one experiences cultural shock depends on a wide variety of factors, some of which are previous familiarity with other cultures, amount of preparations for the cultural change, the availability of support systems, the degree of differences between the native culture and the new one, and differences of individual personalities" (Winkelman, 1994, p. 154).

Immigrants also face other important issues, especially when adjusting to the many losses that accompany immigration. One of these includes the stress of resettlement causing traditional roles to shift, which can contribute to marital discord and conflict, severe psychological stress, feelings of depression, family conflicts, and even domestic abuse (Drachman & Halberstadt, 1992).

Assimilation and Acculturation

Acculturation is the process of acquiring the culture of a society different from one's own, of becoming bicultural, establishing an operative balance between how much of one's own culture one wishes to keep and the extent to which one seeks and supports positive relations with the dominant culture and internalizes the values of that culture. This is the transformation process that occurs when a culturally distinct group or individual comes into contact with another (Berry & Kim, 1988). Cultural identity changes such as language, cultural beliefs, values, and behaviors of the dominant society may occur at this time.

Nilsson, Brown, Russell, and Khamphakdy-Brown (2008) examined the relations among acculturation, domestic violence, and mental health in 62 married women from Somalia who were part of one of the largest ethnic groups in Ethiopia, according to Sullivan, Senturia, Negash, Shiu-Thornton, and Giday (2005)—and the largest group of refugees entering the United States in 2005. According to these researchers, women who reported greater ability to speak English also reported more experiences of psychological and physical abuse from their partners.

Sullivan et al. conducted focus groups with 18 Ethiopian survivors of domestic violence, who reported that domestic violence was common in their communities in both the United States and Ethiopia but the abuse was more openly displayed in Ethiopia. The participants stated that despite the fact that domestic abuse was illegal in the United States, their community did not support the US laws and instead responded to abuse in traditional Ethiopian ways (e.g., supporting the abuser and minimizing the importance of the abuse). According to Darvishpour (2002) and Min (2001), domestic violence may be initiated or exacerbated by resettlement stressors, such as language barriers and cultural differences. Also, the greater the cultural differences between the native and the new culture, the more stress. One common stressor is change in gender roles when resettling in the United States because the women may have to work outside the home for the first time and may end up working more hours and making more money than do their male partners. Resettlement in a westernized country may also provide women from patriarchal societies such as Somalia with positive experiences, such as increased sense of power and independence, while, in contrast, resettlement may lead to unemployment, loss of power and status, and diminished sense of identity for men. This may contribute to and increase marital conflicts and domestic violence. Often, immigrants from traditional societies, including immigrants from Ethiopia in Israel, have become impoverished after immigrating to modern countries because of language barriers and lack of education. Most of the Israeli families of Ethiopian origin, for example, have economic problems due to unemployment (Swirsky & Joseph, 2005).

Studies have shown that domestic violence has detrimental effects, including depression and suicidal ideation, on the victim's emotional health (Fergusson, Horwood, & Ridder, 2005). According to Liao (2006), "Asian Indian women who immigrated to the United States through arranged marriages are at high risk of experiencing domestic abuse" (p. 23). The professionals working with these women were able to identify unique cultural and contextual factors related to abuse experienced by these women, and Liao's article provides a taxonomy of the factors related to the domestic violence they experienced in the United States.

In a study conducted in Sweden, Iranian men were overrepresented among those who were reported for domestic violence. It may be that the combination of pre-migration trauma and emotional turmoil associated with the immigration makes some refugee men resort to violence as a way of reestablishing power and control (Darvishpour, 2002; Friedman, 1992; Min, 2001;). There is also some evidence that the mental health of refugees in general is lower than that of the nonimmigrant population (Porter & Haslam, 2005).

Additionally, a review of the literature relating specifically to spousal violence among people who have immigrated from traditional to modern societies indicates a correlation between the undermining of the old social order and the rise in incidence of violence within their communities. This correlation gains in intensity if the original culture was fundamentally patriarchal (Rianon & Shelton, 2003).

Researchers point out the cultural differences in defining domestic violence. Modern societies refer to spousal abuse as domestic violence, although in some traditional societies, such as that of Ethiopian Jews, life within the framework of extended families may also include violence perpetrated by others—a mother-in-law, for instance (Taylor, Cheers, Weetra, & Gentle, 2004).

As discussed previously, battered women who consider applying for assistance in the western countries to which they have immigrated have to evaluate the implications to their status within their cultural community and the effects on the community as a whole. Consequently, in many cases, they will choose not to apply for help. Other factors also affect their reluctance to apply for help, including language barriers, suspicions, and receiving responses that do not suit their expectations (Bui, 2003).

Inequities in the Job Market

Domestic violence may negatively affect employment outcome, according to researchers Crowne et al. (2011). Their study explored the relationship between intimate partner violence and employment stability, both concurrently and longitudinally among a sample of 512 predominantly Asian American and Pacific Islander women living in Hawaii. The study examined the longitudinal impact of domestic violence by analyzing violence at two time points as predictors of unstable employment six to eight years later. The results showed both concurrent and longitudinal negative associations of intimate partner violence with employment stability. In addition, women who experienced violence were more likely to be experiencing unstable employment at the same time, and women who had experienced intimate partner violence had lower levels of employment stability six years later. This increase was partially mediated when they experienced depressive symptoms. In the (2011) study by Crowne et al., women who identified primarily as Native Hawaiian or Pacific Islander were much more likely to experience unstable employment than were Asian American women.

Research has suggested that the relationship between intimate partner violence and employment is complex; some studies (Meisel,

Chandler, & Rienzi, 2003; Romero, Chavkin, Wise, & Smith, 2003) have found that intimate partner violence is associated with decreased employment, whereas others (Honeycutt et al., 2001; Tolman & Rosen, 2001) suggest that this relationship is not clear. There is strong evidence that those women who are employed and experiencing domestic violence often experience a variety of interference tactics from their abusive partners, including undermining the women's efforts to get to work by hiding or stealing keys or transportation money and by refusing to care for the children (Moe & Bell, 2004; Swanberg, Macke, & Logan, 2006). Women's experience of domestic violence is also associated with increased tardiness, absenteeism, and use of sick days because of injuries, as well as problems with concentration, job performance, and productivity (Brush, 2002; Moe & Bell, 2004; Reeves & O'Leary-Kelly, 2007). Women who are in abusive relationships tend to experience high rates of job loss and turnover and, many times, are forced to quit or are fired (Bell, 2003; Swanberg & Logan, 2005; Swanberg et al., 2006).

The difficulties faced on the job by women as a result of domestic abuse may have long-term effects on their opportunities for stable employment (Riger, Staggs, & Schewe, 2004; Staggs & Riger, 2005), which refers to working consistently and has been measured as a percentage of months worked during a specified period. The above researchers stated that their study "clearly demonstrates an association between concurrent intimate partner violence and employment. Women experiencing one or more physical abuse in the preceding twelve months had more than twice the odds of lower employment stability in the same timeframe in multivariate models." These findings are consistent with some of the previous research (Meisel et al., 2003; Romero et al., 2003).

Abuse and poor health are related and function as obstacles to employment stability. Both domestic abuse and poor physical and mental health have been found to be linked to unemployment, underemployment, chronic dependence on welfare, and lost workplace productivity (Danziger, Kalil, & Anderson, 2000; Staggs & Riger, 2005). The researchers examined how recency and chronicity of violence affect health and employment, using a sample of current and former public assistance recipients to test the hypothesis that health mediates the relationship between abuse and employment stability over time, given that the effects of abuse, combined with the stressors of poverty and welfare reform, may increase the psychological stress response, which can affect both physical and mental health (Campbell, 2002). The study also discovered that poor women experienced significant stress in attempting to obtain steady employment. Finding reliable childcare can be difficult, so women with low levels of education and work experience often have low-wage and unstable jobs that do not offer health insurance. These jobs may provide little opportunity for the women to exert personal control over their work environments or job tasks yet require considerable effort, such as arranging transportation and day care, or dealing with the abuser thwarting and sabotaging her efforts to work. Finally, precarious employment creates job strain, which increases mental and physical stress-related illness in the long term (Lewchuk, de Wolff, King, & Polanyi, 2003).

Effect of Domestic Abuse on Family Structure

According to Liebmann (2012), domestic abuse has both direct and indirect effects on the family structure, including deportations, which separate the family, and neglect, in which the children end up in foster care. Liebmann's study also found that domestic abuse causes changes in families' daily lives, such as limiting going out of their homes, limiting how far they drive from home, not attending events around town because of fears of deportation or of being separated from their families. Liebmann believes that these ongoing fears trigger health issues including high blood pressure, high anxiety, stress and emotional distress in some families. Such health issues can even lead to the high number of deportations that separate families and lead to permanent terminations of parental rights, and the heightened risk faced by survivors of domestic violence of losing their children because of both detention and deportation.

Studies by Abasiubong et al. (2010) and Anitha (2008) focused mostly on domestic violence against pregnant women, whereas researchers Constantino, Kim, and Crane (2005) examined the feasibility and effectiveness of a social support intervention with women while they were in a domestic violence shelter. Health outcomes were examined before and after intervention, using a randomized control design. In this study, domestic violence was defined as violent or controlling behavior by the husband or intimate partner. Intimate partner violence does not respect age, ethnicity, religion, class, identity, ability, immigration status, or educational status, and women are more likely to be assaulted, injured, raped, or killed by current or past partners than any other type of assailant. Pattern of abuse includes physical, sexual, and psychological assault (Seimer, 2004; Wisner, Gilmer, Saltzman, & Zink, 1999).

Another study, by Constantino, Sekula, Rabin, and Stone (2000) focused on the effect of the abuse by the husband when he depended on his wife financially or for other things that would make the process of leaving her difficult. Compounding the issue further are the negative health repercussions of intimate partner violence. Women who are subjected to domestic violence self-report high healthcare utilization, have low general health, and are at risk for poor mental and physical health. They also have higher medical costs than nonabused women because of the increase in physical health problems caused by the abuse (Coid et al., 2003; Constantino et al., 2000).

Abused women are significantly more likely to be hospitalized in the year before filing a protection order, for diagnoses ranging from self-injury, poisoning, and gastrointestinal disorder to assault injuries, psychiatric disorders, and attempted suicide. The signs of psychosocial damage from domestic violence may not be as obvious as physical injury but may have more profound effects.

The significance of various long-term health problems and their associated financial costs are clearly addressed in the literature and indicate a need for development of appropriate interventions and their evaluation (Crandall, Nathens, & Rivara, 2004; Kernic, Wolf, & Holt, 2000; Mayer & Coulter, 2002; Tjaden & Thoennes, 2000; Vogel &

Marshall, 2001). Domestic violence may affect women for a lifetime and have critical effects on families. For example, one-third of all women murder victims were murdered by a current or past intimate partner, a number that remained virtually unchanged from 1993 to 2000 (Rennison & Planty, 2003).

In the United States, intimate partner violence costs $12.6 billion annually in legal and medical services, judicial system costs, and lost productivity. Violence prevention and intervention are considered to be cost effective, a benefit to the safety of the public, and economically sound (Waters et al., 2004; WHO, 1999). Interventions can include abuse screening in acute and primary care settings, referrals, and various treatment interventions for abused women and their perpetrators. Screening interventions are a professional responsibility of healthcare providers. It is not known if screening reduces abuse, but women considered screening for abuse to be an acceptable process when provided in healthcare settings. According to the author, however, few healthcare providers screen for domestic abuse even though it is mandatory in almost all states.

A 2004 review by Nelson, Nygren, McInerney, and Klein of screening and interventions for women assessed how they worked adverse effects and how effective these interventions were at reducing harm or future abuse. The interventions included individual counseling and outreach. The study determined that the severity of violence was lower after two months in the outreach group but not in the counseling group. After six, twelve, and eighteen months' follow-up, however, abuse scores were lower for women in both groups.

Nelson and colleagues conducted a second study (2004), providing counseling in addition to wallet cards with community resources listed. Less violence was reported by women in the counseling intervention group at six and twelve months. The researchers conducted this study after discovering in the first that no extant studies provided information on the adverse effects of screening or intervention, addressed the effectiveness of screening instruments at reducing harm, or evaluated whether interventions improved violence or health outcomes. They therefore aimed another review of intimate partner violence interventions at prevention strategies from primary-care perspectives for detection of intimate partner violence. They reviewed 2,185 abstracts, with 22 articles meeting the reviewers' criteria. The goal of the review was to assess the effectiveness of prevention strategies, usually measured by ongoing abuse, counseling, further visits to the hospital, and improvements in mental health, but the interventions for abused women in the reviewed studies included none of these, only advocacy with a shelter stay, effectiveness of staying in a shelter, prenatal counseling, personal and vocational counseling, and social and policy intervention (Wathen & MacMillan, 2003).

Some studies have shown that social support interventions can be provided in small groups to women experiencing domestic violence while those women are in shelters, to beneficial health effect, because groups may validate the intimate partner experience, reduce the associated stress, improve health outcomes, and contribute to the adaptation process (Cohen & Hoberman, 1983). Researchers Moylan et al. (2009) studied the outcomes of family violence and resilience in individuals and families. The results show that both child abuse and domestic violence increase a child's risk for internalizing and externalizing outcomes in adolescence. Also, when accounting for risk factors associated with additional stressors in the family and surrounding environment, only those children with dual exposure showed high risk of the tested outcomes compared to adolescents who were not exposed to domestic violence. Some observable differences existed in the prediction of outcomes for children with dual exposure compared to those exposed to domestic violence only, however.

The study showed that every year, an estimated 3.3 million to 10 million children are exposed to domestic violence in their homes (Carlson, 1984; Straus, 1999). According to United States Department of Health and Human Services, "Studies investigating the prevalence of child maltreatment by parents and other caretakers." Different forms of family violence often co-occur, suggesting that many children who witness domestic violence have also directly experienced child abuse

(Edleson, 2001; Tajima, 2004). Multiple studies have demonstrated that children who have been exposed to both domestic violence and child abuse are more likely to experience a wide range of adverse psychosocial and behavioral outcomes, so these researchers have posited what they call "double whammy," or dual-exposure effect, in which children exposed to both child abuse and domestic violence fare worse with respect to later outcomes than do those exposed only to one form of violence (Moylan et al., 2009; Sternberg et al., 2006; Wolfe et al., 2003). The effects of being abused persist into adolescence with the relationship between domestic abuse exposure and adverse psychosocial outcomes. Exposure to domestic abuse in childhood has been linked low self-esteem, social withdrawal, depression, and anxiety.

A recent analysis of studies examining the relationship between domestic violence exposure in childhood and adolescent internalizing and externalizing behaviors found significant mean weighted effect sizes of .48 (SE = .04) for internalizing behaviors and .47 (SE = .05) for externalizing behaviors, indicating moderate associations between exposure and both outcomes (Edleson, 2001; Lichter & McCloskey, 2004; Litrownik, Newton, Hunter, English, & Everson, 2003; Moffitt, Caspi, & Rutter, 2005; Suermann, 1997). Evidence of "double whammy" effects has been demonstrated by several studies examining the dual-exposure hypothesis, finding that children who were direct victims of abuse and also exposed to domestic abuse had higher externalizing scores than did those who only witnessed domestic violence (Hughes, 1988).

According to Richards (2011), research has demonstrated that a substantial amount of domestic violence is witnessed by children and has been recognized as a form of child abuse, both in the United States and internationally. Richards (2011) indicates that children may witness and experience domestic violence in a number of ways, including hearing the violence, being forced to watch or participate in assaults, being used as a physical weapon, being forced to spy on a parent, being informed that he or she is to blame for the violence, being used as a hostage, and intervening to stop the violence. All these incidents have psychological, behavioral, health, and socioeconomic effects on family structure. Children who live in homes characterized by violence between parents or by violence directed at one parent by another have therefore been called the silent, forgotten, unintended, invisible, and secondary victims of domestic violence (Edleson, 2001; Kovacs & Tomison, 2003).

During the past decade, domestic abuse has become a major concern not only for law enforcement officers but also for social policy, health care, and education. According to researcher Woodtli (2000), domestic violence is a major social, health, legal, and educational issue confronting all segments of society and is one from which nurse educators are not immune, meaning that the rush to "do something" has resulted in an inordinate number of research studies, programs, interventions, and strategies that often are fragmented and lack communication links among the various groups involved.

Similarly, nursing education has often responded in a some-what fragmented manner in an attempt to provide students with the knowledge and skills needed to care for domestic abuse victims. Researchers found programs with reading assignments, and programs with varying amounts and types of information about woman, child, and elder abuse. Despite evidence that educational intervention positively affects nurses' responses to domestic violence, there seems to be no consensus on integration of violence- related content and experiences into nursing curricula (Tilden et al., 1994). McBride and Campbell (1998) recognized the need for attention in the nursing curriculum to the problems of domestic violence. They also noted that violence against women was a relatively invisible curriculum topic and urged that it be viewed as a major area of study in future nursing education programs. Both the American Nurses Association (1991) and the American Academy of Nurses (1993) issued papers and position statements on violence and relationship to nursing practice and, by implication, to nursing education (McBride & Campbell, 1998).

Domestic violence also affects social and health status by affecting immigrant women's mobility within the community or neighborhood because of the women's fear of being arrested and deported, which then affects their use of health care, such as regular doctor's visits, diabetes education classes, vaccines, prenatal care, HIV education programs, and appropriate medications. Health issues such as high blood pressure and stress can result from insufficient use of health resources (Hardy et al., 2012).

According to researchers Hardy et al. (2012), immigrants overwhelmingly suffer disproportionate health consequences because of racial and ethnic disparities, and stringent immigration policies and enforcement practices could exacerbate these disparities. However, a recent study by Umoh, Abah, Ugege, and Inyangetoh (2012) focused on the effects of spousal abuse in pregnancy as a major public health and human rights concern. The study identified the prevalence of spousal abuse in pregnant women and identified the women's attitudes toward this phenomenon in their environment as the key to developing strategies for effective intervention. The studied found that spousal physical violence in pregnancy is common in Uyo in the Delta region of Nigeria, at all education levels, which shows that a significant proportion of women still condone domestic abuse and even find excuses for such acts, and that it is therefore important to develop strategies to enlighten women on the unacceptability of violence against women in general and in pregnant women in particular.

Cycle of Violence

The three phases of Lenore Walker's cycle of violence model (1984) are the tension-building phase, the acute battering incident phase, and the honeymoon phase. Each of these phases is very noticeable in abusive relationships.

In the first phase, the tension-building phase, physical and verbal abuse are minimal. The woman usually attempts to soothe her partner to make him less angry, but she is rarely successful. Next will come the acute battering incident phase, when the man becomes extremely violent after the woman has failed to "placate" him. During this phase, the woman receives the worst of the physical and verbal violence. The final phase is the honeymoon phase, during which the man tends to show remorse for how he has treated the woman. He will convince her that he loves her and that he will never abuse her again. He will also tend to meet all of her needs and will buy her gifts, hoping that these actions will make her forget how he has treated her. After the man does all these good deeds for her, the woman is convinced that he actually does love her and he has changed for the better, and she does not know that the cycle will only continue.

Phase 1: Tension Building

In this phase, the abuser may be extremely critical, bullying, and demanding. The victim may still feel some control over the situation and have several chances to pacify the abuser and prevent the next phase. Because of an increase in tension, however, these attempts may not be effective.

Ngozi, a 45-year-old battered woman, described this tension-building phase as she experienced it. She said at first her husband would become very upset for no reason; he would also be very abusive and would start complaining about the food and other things in the house. She would try to calm him down by saying, "Okay, if you don't like it, I will cook another food." During this time, he would become more enraged and demanding, so she would stop trying, so he would not become angrier. Ngozi should have sought outside help at this time, but she did not.

Phase 2: Battering

In this phase, the abuser becomes more physically and emotionally violent, which leads to the victim feeling completely helpless. During this stage, the victim may need to seek appropriate medical attention and safe shelter.

Mary, a 35-year-old abused victim, stated, "My husband became very physically and emotionally abusive. He started biting me and calling me stupid. I fell in one attempt to flee from him. I broke my hand and had to go to the emergency room. From there I was placed in a shelter for my safety. I thank God that my kids were still back in Nigeria with my parents."

Phase 3: Honeymoon

In this phase, the abuser may repeatedly express regret or appear to be remorseful.

Ngozi stated, "During this time I became very confused because my husband will feel very horrible and [feel] remorse about everything. Then he would shower me with gifts and promise that he will never do it again and even go to counseling. I will think that he really means it and thank God that the violence is over. I believed everything he said, not knowing that it is all manipulation and that he will repeat the violent behavior."

Possible Solutions to Domestic Violence

Studies by Bartels (2011) and Kishor and Johnson (2005) show that domestic abuse has become a major problem. One of the possible solutions to this problem is the use of perpetrator programs designed to help men change their abusive behaviors and avoid the possible recurrence of domestic violence.

In the same manner, economic barriers are not the only ones that immigrant women face. Immigrant women, unlike citizens, often may not legally work and may face a constant threat of deportation by their abuser (Abraham, 2000; Disrupt, 1998; Narayan, 1995). Abusers of immigrant women often use immigration-related threats to assert power and control over these women. The abuser, if he is a US citizen or a permanent resident, typically uses this power by threatening to have the victim deported by reporting her undocumented status to the

Immigration and Naturalization Service (INS), threatening to revoke her residency sponsorship, or refusing to file necessary immigration petitions that would provide her with lawful citizen status. Dutton, Orloff, and Aguilar Hass (2000) found that 72.3 percent of the battered Latinas they surveyed reported that their spouses never filed immigration petitions for them even though 50.8 percent of the victims qualified to have petitions filed on their behalf. In addition, those abusers who did eventually file petitions for their spouses took almost four years to do so.

Fear of deportation is a very powerful tool used by abusers to prevent battered immigrant women from seeking help and to keep them in violent relationships. Constable (2012) cites as an example a 62-year-old wife who was treated as a slave and physically and sexually abused by her husband but who could not report that abuse because of fear of deportation.

In response to research identifying high rates of undetected domestic violence, health services have responded primarily by providing domestic violence training to healthcare providers and introducing the practice of routine inquiry and screening in order to better identify victims (Ellsberg, 2006; Plichta, 2007). According to Howard, Trevillion, and Agnew-Davies (2010), identification is not enough, however, and effective responses to domestic violence in women requires health services to engage in cross-sector collaboration, particularly because many of the services available for victimized women lie outside the health system, including non- government, legal, and housing sectors. Yet the health sector has been relatively slow to engage with the coordinated community response to domestic violence, despite calls for health services to make stronger links with community-based domestic violence services (Ramsay, Feder, & Rivas, 2005; Thurston & Eisener, 2006). In 2005, the WHO recognized domestic violence as a public health issue, as domestic violence takes a toll on women's physical and mental health (Bonomi et al., 2009; Martin et al., 2002).

Perpetrator Programs

In a 2003 study, Laing reviewed the effectiveness of perpetrator programs in several studies. She determined that it is difficult to come to a conclusive answer regarding the effectiveness of the programs because the studies had varied outcomes—particularly those using experimental methodologies. On the whole, she noted, the perpetrator programs are generally important in the deterrence of domestic violence, but she implied that more research is needed to determine whether the programs are effective.

The researcher addressed and examined programs, such as educational and support groups, to motivate and encourage women who are afraid to report domestic abuse. According to researchers Hamilton, Koehler, and Losel (2012), most research on domestic violence perpetrator programs has been carried out in North America. Because the research did not yet provide a clear picture about what really works with these offenders and cannot be generalized to other cultural and legal systems, Hamilton, Koehler, and Losel conducted a survey in European countries to address the practice and effect of perpetrator programs. They found that most programs applied cognitive-behavioral treatment, psychodynamic treatment, and combinations of treatment types. There was a wide variety of approaches to handling domestic violence perpetrators, as well a particular dearth of high-quality evaluation throughout the continent; however, recent estimates of the lifetime prevalence of domestic violence among European women reports that roughly 12–16 percent of women throughout the continent have experienced an episode of physical abuse at the hands of a partner at or after the age of 16 (Council of Europe, 2008). Domestic violence victimization has been associated with an increased likelihood of substance abuse, depression, posttraumatic stress, suicidal ideation, injury, and death (Alhabib, Nur, & Jones, 2010; Campbell, 2002).

Gondolf (2002) found that there were three prevailing approaches to domestic violence perpetrator programs—cognitive- behavioral, psychodynamic, and profeminist—and that they have limited and mixed support. My own studies show that cognitive-behavioral programs attribute violence to learned behaviors that perform an expressive, instrumental function and these programs consequently emphasize that desistance must be learned through a process of cognitive restructuring. Psychodynamic approaches emphasize the personality and emotional disposition of the perpetrator as being central to desistance, by facilitating the recognition and reconciliation of latent feelings of emasculation that precipitated the abusive impulses. Profeminist approaches view violence as originating from patriarchal values about women's roles and typically aim to reorient the way men exert power and control over their partners.

Even though other treatment approaches to dealing with domestic violence perpetrators exist, they are difficult to find (Barnish, 2004). In spite of this, recent advances have provided some good suggestions for the possible differentiation of treatment approaches to correspond more closely with variations along observed situational, cultural, and psychological dimensions such as gender-role and comorbid disorders (Gilchrist & Kebbell, 2010; Graham-Kevan, 2007; Mcmurran & Gilchrist, 2008). According to researcher Fisher (2011), perpetrator programs in Ireland are delivered through a combination of nongovernmental bodies and probation services, and since the 1980s, there has been a network for perpetrator programs that aims at changing the abusive behaviors of male perpetrators by a combination of charitable and voluntary contributions and state funding. Fisher carefully observed both the victims and the perpetrators involved in these programs to ensure the safety of the victims and their families, but to date, not enough evidence demonstrates the effectiveness of the programs.

Madoc-Jones and Roscoe (2010) focused on services provided for women victims of domestic violence—mainly those who were attending a group in a domestic violence program in the probation department in the United Kingdom. The study focused on women because the participants interviewed for this research were all women and were all victims of domestic violence according to the criminal justice system. In 2006, Hague and Mullender pointed out that the voices of women who have experienced domestic violence are rarely heard by both professionals and the criminal justice system. For example, one of the women who expressed feelings of abandonment by the criminal justice system stated, "He had probation, his solicitor and everyone helping him with his problems, but until women services came along, no one seemed interested in me. There was no one at all for me." Madoc-Jones and Roscoe therefore addressed that silence by exploring the services offered to women when their abusers attended the Integrated Domestic Abuse Program (IDAP) because of a court-mandated order or because they are in prison in the UK. Domestic violence is a significant criminal justice and social policy issue, and the scale of the problem is well documented worldwide. Because it is estimated that one in four women in the UK will experience some form of domestic violence at some point in their lives (Coleman et al., 2007; Hague & Mullender, 2006; Harwin, 2006), since 2003, the Correctional Services Accreditation Panel has required each of the 43 probation areas in England and Wales to exclusively deliver either the IDAP or the Community Domestic Violence Program (CVDP). As of 2008, 34 probation areas provided the IDAP and 9 provided the CVDP (National Probation Services, 2008).

Other studies show that domestic violence is widely recognized as a major social problem in Australia, in which it was estimated that approximately 5 percent of the population are victimized in any one year. International surveys suggest that about one-third of all women will experience abuse perpetrated by an intimate male partner at some point in their lives (Access Economics, 2004; Coulter & VandeWeerd, 2009). Often, the abuse associated with domestic violence is serious. Most of the incidents involve physical injuries, and approximately two-thirds of the women who are murdered are killed by their husbands or live-in partners. The most recent Australian statistics on homicide show that of the 113 homicides involving female victims reported in 2005–2006, more than half (n = 66) followed arguments related to domestic disputes (Davies & Mouzos, 2007). Australian research on male perpetrator intervention programs has been largely confined to policy, procedural, and organizational analysis, but few data for the effects of the interventions have been examined (O'Leary, Chung, & Zannettino, 2004).

In a similar study, Mullender and Burton (2001) indicated that 67 percent of the perpetrators coming into the programs were able to avoid further violence after leaving the programs; however, the study claimed that the figure eventually declined, with only a few responding positively to the program. Mullender and Burton's study also considered the performance of programs in African countries, but the programs in these countries had the same disappointing results, with only a few perpetrators returning for the second stage of the program. As Mullender and Burton pointed out, interventions with domestic violence perpetrators are fraught with difficulties because there is a danger that unless the work is well thought through, it will either fail to address the real needs of violent men or will place some women in greater danger.

Status Issues

Domestic violence can take numerous patterns: physical, psychological, emotional, financial, and spiritual. Suppression of women against their will constitutes a form of control and domination. Previous studies conducted in this area show a variety of social, cultural, and material factors—such as low social status of women, patriarchal attitudes, early marriage, alcoholism, education, gender-role socialization, and income disparity—associated with male abuse of women. Knowledge and proper identification of the diversity of the experiences of domestic violence among women will help stem the tide of this problem among women and will also help in addressing the needs of abused women from diverse socio- cultural backgrounds in meaningful ways (Dobash & Dobash, 1983; Isiugo-Abanihe, 2003; Isiugo-Abanihe and Oyedrian, 2003; Nwokocha, 2004).

Summary

I studied domestic violence against Nigerian women living in Southern California (Los Angeles, San Bernardino, Orange, and San Diego Counties). According to Brownridge (2002), in the past few decades, the issue of domestic violence has been a major focus of research and policy; studies have shown that it is a global issue that negatively affects the social and health status of individuals and of women in particular.

Although current literature advocates for an understanding of diverse experiences of domestic violence and complex experiences of black immigrant women in Canada (Cousineau & Rondeau, 2004), there is a lack of literature on Nigerian American women's experiences of domestic violence. My research was thus motivated by the desire to fill that gap, highlight the root causes of this problem, and discover the significant role played by the cultural differences in perpetuating the problem. This study also aimed to develop appropriate sociocultural programs to assist Nigerian American women in abusive relationships, as well as to inform social policies that would direct attitudes and behaviors toward a culturally inclusive society.

CHAPTER 3

Methodology

The primary method employed in this research study was in- depth interviews (see Appendix A) guided by a qualitative research framework. This afforded Nigerian American woman the opportunity to voice their opinions and talk about their personal experiences of domestic violence in their own words. It was my intent to conduct the interviews within June 2014. These interviews were conducted in the major cities of Southern California (Los Angeles, San Bernardino, Orange, and San Diego Counties), specifically because these cities are home to a very large number of Nigerians. Southern California contains roughly 60 percent of California's approximately 38 million people (USC Journal, 2008). At the time of this study, however, the percentage of Californians who were Nigerians had not yet been established, however. This issue is addressed under limitations of the study.

Research Questions

This study focused on the significant role of culture in domestic violence among Nigerian women living in Southern California. Two research questions drove the study of this cross-section of the population. I intended to examine both culture and employment conditions of immigrants, then derive valid conclusions based on the following research questions and hypotheses:

1. What are the perceptions of Nigerian women living in Southern California about the significant role of culture and employment conditions on domestic violence in the Nigerian community?
    a. What is the role of cultural factors contributing to domestic violence (Q9a)?
    b. What systemic factors contribute to abuse?
    c. What factors affect women's ability to seek help and services?
2. Do Nigerian American women who self-identify as victims of intimate partner violence (IPV) accept cultural differences and employment conditions as a basis of domestic abuse and therefore not seek assistance for this problem?

Directional Hypothesis: There is a perception among Nigerian women living in Southern California about the significant role of culture on domestic violence.

Null Hypothesis: There is no substantial perception among Nigerian women living in Southern California about the significant role of culture and employment conditions on domestic violence.

Study Sample

I looked for respondents who had lived in Southern California from five to twelve years, and I projected that all respondents I would interview would be women who worked outside the home, with estimated annual incomes ranging between $15,000 and $110,000. The respondents' occupations included housekeeper, teacher, social worker, lawyer, engineer, housewife, healthcare professional, and insurance agent.

The study sample consisted of five first-generation Nigerian American women, some married and some divorced, from various

Nigerian states and ethnicities, as well as some key participants from local Nigerian associations who were living in Southern California and were very familiar with issues and concerns in the Nigerian community living there. The respondents' ages ranged from 25 to 45 years. Most of the women were formally educated, with academic backgrounds ranging from high school to higher education. Respondents had been married from 10 to 30 years.

Study Questions

The interview questions were framed in a manner that allowed the respondents to describe their experiences freely, without any consideration of the quality of the information provided. In addition to the sociodemographic characteristics of the respondents, the questions covered subjects such as respondents' histories, experiences of migration, family composition and dynamics, experiences of violence in Nigeria and in the United States, and views on the types of intervention that would effectively address abuse of women.

Data Collection

Initial contact was with the five Nigerian women who were currently married to Nigerian men or had been married but were divorced and lived in Southern California. Participants were recommended and referred by acquaintances in the Nigerian community in Southern California. The participants were chosen by personal contact via telephone. This survey was in the form of a questionnaire with ten questions.

The method of survey was face-to-face-interview (see Appendix A). The physical location was the local library or some other venue where the participants felt comfortable and safe enough to be interviewed.

In line with ethical requirements for human-based studies, respondents' actual names were not used; rather, pseudonyms were used. The data were stored in a safe, locked up in my home. After the study was complete, the documents were retained for six months and then shredded.

Data Analysis

Because of the nature of this project and limited available literature in this area of study, the major purpose of the research was to increase understanding of the effects of cultural differences on Nigerian women in abusive relationships in Southern California. Data collected were uniquely analyzed using a manual process. Data were carefully collated and compiled so that respondents' answers, views, and concerns were highlighted to reflect their opinions and understanding of culture's role in their respective abusive relationships. Special attention was given to information collected and its patterns, context, and meanings as they relate to the subject matter and future studies to be conducted in this field. This method of data analysis emphasized both the commonality and differences of interviewees' experiences in understanding in particular occurrences the potential role that culture plays in domestic violence among Nigerian women in Southern California.

All cultural factors provided in respondents' answers were properly and carefully analyzed to reflect the extent of their perception of culture's role in domestic violence. Other vital issues such as parenting, disparity in finances, upbringing, family values, culturally prescribed gender role, and relational problems were considered. I divided the findings from this study into three main sections: (1) role of cultural factors contributing to domestic violence, (2) systemic factors contributing to abuse, and (3) factors affecting women's ability to seek help and services.

Timeline

The timeline for this research study was six to eight months. The survey and interview process was projected to both begin and conclude in June

2014. Three months were allowed for data collection and analysis. The reporting of findings were planned to take approximately one month.

Research Key Words

Domestic violence, domestic abuse, role of culture, and *employment conditions in domestic violence.*

Definitions of Terms

Culture: Attributes or characteristics of ways in which a particular group of people or individuals behave or act.

Domestic abuse: Domestic violence, spousal abuse, child abuse, or intimate partner violence; can be broadly defined and can be used interchangeably with any of these individual terms.

Domestic violence: Violence or physical abuse directed toward a spouse or domestic partner, usually violence by men against women, though it can also include violence by women against men.

Employment conditions: Terms and conditions under which noncitizens can be gainfully employed or rewarded for exchange of their services.

CHAPTER 4

Results

The prevalence and influence of domestic abuse of Nigerian women living in Southern California creates fear, anxiety, and loss of hope among middle-class women. In Nigeria, women are not expected to pay bills and taxes, because all family expenses are incurred by men. Most of the Nigerian women coming to the United States had high hopes for more successful lives than they had back home. Most expected to work and earn reasonable incomes, but some have been disappointed by low-paying jobs with meager salaries. In contrast, some of the men are unwilling to change the standards to which they were accustomed, preventing their wives from working and forcing them to remain perpetual housewives under tight control of their husbands. These men become abusive while working more than one job to provide for the entire family.

This new way of life forces the abused women to be submissive to their husbands to the point that they will not report abuse to the authorities because of fear of punishment by their abusive husbands (Nworah, 2010). This type of environment helps to promote domestic abuse and suppresses the women's ability to live like their host counterparts. Some of these women are prevented from getting good-paying jobs because of fear of abuse, fear of deportation, financial hardship, fear of being blamed for their husbands' arrest, and shame and harassment by friends and extended family; they therefore rely solely on their abusive husbands to provide for them. This situation lends itself to dependency and unnecessary control, which are byproducts of domestic violence (Hardy et al., 2012).

Moreover, some of these women experience issues of unemployment, lack of social support, and institutional discrimination, hampering the women's ability to progress professionally, consequently affecting their domestic lives and eventually resulting in an increased tendency for domestic violence (Anitha, 2008).

This study focused on the significant role of culture in domestic violence among Nigerian women living in Southern California. I intended to examine both culture and employment conditions of Nigerian immigrants and then derive valid conclusions based on the following two research questions, which were spawned from theory:

1. What are the perceptions of Nigerian women living in Southern California about the significant role of culture and employment conditions on domestic violence in the Nigerian community?
   a. What is the role of cultural factors contributing to domestic violence?
   b. What systemic factors contribute to abuse?
   c. What factors affect women's ability to seek help and services?
2. Do Nigerian American women who self-identify as victims of intimate partner violence (IPV) accept cultural differences and employment conditions as a basis of domestic abuse and therefore not seek assistance for this problem?

This chapter is organized into three major sections. The first section includes information about how participants were interviewed, along with descriptive data about each participant. The second section provides a detailed breakdown of the themes extracted from the interviews by research question. Finally, the third section presents a comprehensive discussion of findings.

Demographics

The aim of this research was to investigate the role of culture on domestic violence among Nigerian women in Southern California. Data collected were analyzed using a manual process. Data were collated and compiled in such a manner that respondents' answers, views, and concerns were highlighted to reflect their opinions and understanding of culture's role in their respective abusive relationships. Special attention was given to the patterns, context, and meanings of the information as they relate to the subject matter.

Table 1 presents a summary of respondents' basic demographic information, including age, year of transition to the United States, and age of transition. In addition, all individuals were given pseudonyms to protect their identities. As evidenced by the table, seven of fifteen were at least 45 years old, while eight reported being between the ages of 36 and 45 years. The earliest transition to the United States was in 1982, and the latest was in 2008. Similarly, the youngest age at transition was 16, whereas the oldest was

46 years.

Table 1

General Demographic Data for All Participants

Case	Pseudonym	Age	Year of Transition	Age at Transition
1	Abby	45+	2000	32
2	Brenda	45+	2001	46
3	Cara	45+	2005	25
4	Donna	45+	1982	32
5	Eve	36–45	2008	32
6	Fran	36–45	2000	32
7	Gabby	36–45	2001	46
8	Heather	36–45	2005	25
9	Isabelle	36–45	1982	32
10	Jackie	36–45	2008	32
11	Katie	36–45	1998	16
12	Lindy	45+	2002	32
13	Monica	45+	2002	26
14	Nicole	45+	2004	40
15	Olivia	36–45	2004	30

Note: N = 15

Qualitative Results

Research Question 1a

Research question 1a (*What is the role of cultural factors contributing to domestic violence?*) was answered via two interview questions: questions 9 and 9a. The first question in this series was question 9 (*Do you believe cultural factors contribute to domestic violence?*)

All 15 of the women interviewed reported that culture is a factor contributing to domestic violence. Table 2 displays the interview question, along with the frequency of responses.

Table 2

Culture as a Factor That Contributes to Domestic Violence Frequency

Question	Response Option	Frequency
Do you believe cultural factors contribute to domestic violence?	Yes	15
	No	0

Interview question 9a asked, *How does patriarchy in the culture contribute to the violence?* Of the 15 Nigerian women who were interviewed, 11 answered this question. One major theme and three minor themes were extracted from the interviews. All 11 of the women who responded reported that male dominance was the most influential, if not the only, factor contributing to domestic violence.

For example, Abby reported, "Patriarchy in the culture contributes a lot [to] the violence because of men dominating the women, with the mentality that they are the *authority* over their wives."

Additionally, Katie stated, "Patriarchy allows males [to] hold *primary power* in their household and society, which gives them more power, and this contributes to the increase of domestic violence."

Monica reported, "The Nigerian culture tend[s] to see the man as a *superior* head of the home, the one who makes the final decision, so attempts for the woman to change that may seem as *rebellious* or disrespectful, which can lead to domestic violence."

Table 3 displays the interview question, along with frequency of responses.

Table 3

Thematic Response to Interview Question 9a

Question	Theme	Frequency
How does patriarchy in the culture contribute to the violence?	Male dominance	11
	Culture gives men more authority	2
	Culture sees men as superior	2
	Culture portrays women as rebellious	1

All 15 participants felt that cultural factors played a significant role in contributing to domestic violence. They generally felt that males dominating females was the main reason, and that the cultural belief that males hold final authority and are superior led to women being portrayed as rebellious if they disobeyed.

Research Question 1b

Research question 1b (*What systemic factors contribute to abuse?*) was answered via two interview questions: interview questions 6c and 6d. The first question in this series was question 6c (*How did moving to the United States impact your family?*)

Of the 15 women interviewed, 13 responded to this question. Two (2) reported that moving had no impact, and 11 reported that moving to the United States affected their families emotionally. In the majority of the cases (7 of 11), the women reported that the move led to some sort of abusive behavior from their husbands. Eve, Jackie, Lindsay, Nicole, and Olivia all reported multiple factors of anger, abuse, stress, and even financial stressors. Specifically, Eve stated, "His behavior of verbal abuse and anger at all times really affected our family."

Additionally, Abby stated, "By daily argument, ... my partner became defensive and verbally abusive at all times."

Olivia stated, "My husband did not really like the fact that he has to file for me so I can have a job as a lawyer and I have to take another exam in this country to be able to practice. This developed financial issues in which he became angry at all time[s]."

Table 4 displays the interview question, along with the frequency of responses.

Table 4

Thematic Responses to Interview Question 6c

Question 6c	Themes	Frequency
How did [the move] impact your family?	Main Theme	
	Emotional effect	11
	No effect	2
	Subtheme	
	Anger	5
	Abuse	7
	Stress	1
	Financial issues	1

Of the 15 women who were interviewed, 13 responded to interview question 6d. Two reported that moving had no impact, while 11 of them reported that moving to the United States affected their families emotionally. Specifically, four major themes were extracted from the data. In five of the cases, the women reported emotional separation between them and their husbands, and four reported that abuse occurred. Abby and Fran reported multiple factors, both *separation* and *abuse*.

Emotionally, Abby stated, "The relationship became very distant and abusive."

Lindsay replied that the relationship between her and her husband became "really negative and abusive."

A couple of the other women, including Katie and Nicole, expressed *lack of support* and *fear* of their husbands once they moved to the United States.

Table 5 displays the interview question, along with the frequency of responses.

Table 5

Thematic Responses to Interview Question 6d

Question 6d	Themes	Frequency
How did [the move] impact your relationship with your husband?	Abuse	4
	Separation	5
	Lack of support	1
	Fear	
	No effect	2

Note: Abby and Fran reported multiple themes.

The interviewed women generally felt that moving to the United States was a very emotional event. The systemic factors that contributed to abuse included abuse, anger, fear, lack of support, stress, and financial problems.

Research Question 1c

Research question 1c (*What factors affect women's ability to seek help and services?*) was answered via a single interview question: interview question 7. Interview question 7 asked, *Can you discuss any external and internal conflicts during this time?*

Of the 15 women interviewed, 13 responded to this question. Three themes were extracted from the interviews: (1) fear to communicate, (2) work-life balance, and (3) argumentativeness. The majority of the women (8 of 13) reported being afraid to communicate with their husbands, with the anticipation of making their husbands very angry. Respondents also reported struggling to balance work and personal life (n = 3), and their relationships with their husbands becoming very argumentative (n = 2), which could also hinder a woman from seeking help outside the home.

Specifically, Olivia stated, "It was a struggle because I could not tell him how I feel so he does not become more angry."

Additionally, Donna reported, "The external and internal conflicts were mostly constant arguments and fighting. I went through the mental struggle because I could not really express my feelings due to his anger and yelling."

Lindsay described the situation like this: "It was challenging to balance work and being a wife and mother."

Table 6 displays the interview question, along with the frequency of responses.

Table 6

Thematic Responses to Interview Question 7

Question 7	Themes	Frequency
Can you discuss any external or internal conflicts during this time?	Fear to communicate	8
	Work-life balance	3
	Argumentativeness	2

Three themes were extracted regarding interview question 1c. The main theme was fear to communicate and was perhaps the most relevant factor affecting women's ability to seek help and services—that is, 8 of the interviewed Nigerian American women reported fear from retaliation from their husband as the salient theme.

Research Question 2

Research question 2 (*Do Nigerian American women who self-identify as victims of intimate partner violence (IPV) accept cultural differences and employment conditions as a basis of domestic abuse and therefore not seek assistance for this problem?*) was answered via three interview questions: interview questions 6a, 6b, and 10a were constructed to answer this question. The first question in this series was question 6a: *Did you work outside the home when you came to the United States?*

Of the 15 women who were interviewed, 14 responded to this question. One (1) reported that she did not begin to work outside the home when she moved to the United States, whereas 13 reported they had to find work to help support their families. Table 7 displays the interview question, along with the frequency of responses.

Table 7

Frequency of Responses to Question 6a by Response Option

Question 6a	Response Option	Frequency
Did you work outside the home when you came to the United States?	Yes	13
	No	1

The next question in this series was interview question 6b: How was the experience [*of working in the United States] different for you?* Of the 15 women interviewed, 14 responded to this question. Of those 14, three (3) reported there was no difference.

From the responses to interview question 6b, four themes were found. That is, the majority of women reported that the transition from Nigeria to the United States and having to go to work was very difficult, and some of them (n = 5) reported that the transition triggered anger from their husbands. Some of the women (n = 2) reported that it was difficult because they had to try to find childcare, whereas back in Nigeria, family members and in-laws had helped with the children if needed.

For example, Donna reported, "I had to find a babysitter, but back in Nigeria, the relatives and in-laws assisted with the childcare."

Fran stated, "All the expectations and promises about [the] US was not reality, which triggered anger in my home and my partner."

Eve also said, "The expectation that he will continue to support the household became a nightmare."

Table 8 displays the interview question, along with the frequency of responses.

Table 8

Thematic Response to Interview Question 6b

Question 6b	Response Option	Frequency
How was the experience different for you?	Triggered anger	2
	Difficult	5
	Needed childcare	2
	Nightmare	2
	No change	3

The final question used to answer research question 2 was interview question 10a: *Do you think acculturation contributed to the challenges in the home?*

Of the 15 women interviewed, 11 responded to this question. One (1) reported that acculturation did not contribute to the challenges in the home. The other 10 reported that the acculturation process did have an effect on the challenges they faced once they had moved from Nigeria to the United States. In the majority of the cases (6 of 10), the women reported that the acculturation process led to anger and to their fear of violence and of seeking help.

Monica stated, "It is a possibility [that] the role of culture contributes to ... me [not] seeking help from external services. The culture also affects my ability to seek help."

Additionally, Olivia reported, "Yes, acculturation contributed to challenges, and one of the factors was fear of seeking help from external services for domestic violence because [of] the cultural expectations."

Lindsay reported, "Yes. Most of the factors that affected my desire to seek help were because of the culture and fear of getting my husband angry. The culture plays a big role [in] domestic violence."

Table 9 displays the interview question, along with the frequency of responses.

Table 9

Thematic Response to Interview Question 10a

Question 10a	Response Option	Frequency
Do you think acculturation contributed to the challenges in the home?	Yes	10
	Fear of seeking help	6
	Culture and values	4
	No	1

Results from the investigation found that the Nigerian American women interviewed who self-identified as victims of IPV believed that acculturation did contribute to the challenges in their homes. More than half of the respondents attributed their decision to not seek help to fear of retaliation from their husbands.

Summary

The majority of women interviewed felt that the acculturation process and the adjustment of their roles from stay-at-home wives and mothers to working wives and mothers significantly contributed to the violence within their relationships with their husbands. The majority of the women reported keeping their feelings to themselves for fear of making their husbands angry. Fear of making their husbands angry also seemed to be a significant factor in why they did not seek professional help for domestic violence.

CHAPTER 5

Implications and Recommendations

D omestic violence is described as "a pattern of abusive behaviour which escalates in frequency and severity over time" (Bartels, 2005, p. 1). According to this definition, domestive violence is not onetime abuse but abuse that repeats, establishing a pattern that spirals into extreme outcomes, such as severe physical injuries and even death. Laws protecting women and children from this crime have been ratified and implemented in many countries. A study by Kishor and Johnson (2005) reported, "Violence against women, committed by an intimate partner is an important public health and human rights issue." According to these authors, "recent research has focused on intimate partner violence during pregnancy due to its prevalence, adverse health consequences, and intervention potential" (p. 259). The authors discovered that women in countries in which men are the decision makers for the household, such as Cambodia, Colombia, the Dominican Republic, Egypt, Haiti, India, Nicaragua, Peru, and Zambia, experience domestic violence from their spouses regardless of their physical state. This implies that the women in these countries receive abuse even during pregnancy. Generally, such abuse is detrimental to the health and rights of women as well as to the development of the individual nations.

Summary of Results

Research Question 1a

Research question 1a asked, *What is the role of cultural factors contributing to domestic violence?* Based on results from the qualitative analysis, all 15 participants felt that cultural factors played a significant role in contributing to domestic violence. They generally felt that Nigerian culture drove males to dominate females and gave males final authority in the home. This fact led women to be portrayed by other members of their culture as rebellious if they disobeyed, and the combination gave women no recourse or options to help resolve family problems.

Research Question 1b

The women interviewed generally felt that moving to the United States was a very emotional event, and the systemic factors contributing to their abuse included abuse, anger, fear, lack of support, stress, and financial problems.

Research Question 1c

Research question 3 asked, *What systemic factors contribute to abuse?* From the interviews, three themes were extracted in response to this question The main theme was fear to communicate and was perhaps the most relevant factor affecting women's ability to seek help and services. Eight (8) of the 15 women reported fear of retaliation from their husbands as the salient theme.

Research Question 2

Results from the investigation found that acculturation did not contribute to the women's challenges [abuse] in the home. More than half of the respondents attributed fear of retaliation from their husbands as the reason why they did not seek help for their abuse.

Implications

Domestic violence against women is a serious societal issue (Nasir & Hyder, 2003; Neggers et al., 2004), and the cultural disposition toward and stigma attached to violence seem to vitiate the basic human rights of women in the Niger Delta region, making it impossible for women to seek help. Societal sanctions against them seeking help include fear of disownment by family, rejection by friends, and loneliness. This premise was found to be quite evident in the Nigerian American women interviewed in this study. Remarkably, the transition from Nigeria to America may exacerbate the issue and cause women to become even more isolated and afraid. The implications appear rather severe, given the reflections recorded in the interviews. That is, separation, anger, and fear were components associated with the cultural shift. Clearly, these families did not expect or plan for separation, anger, and fear were. The findings from this study provide a rather grim outlook and surely demonstrate that any hope for a better life for these women is squashed, despite the prevalence of wealth and success that dance just out of reach.

Recommendation for Research

Researchers should investigate how acculturation training may mitigate the despair and loneliness that Nigerian women feel after transitioning to the United States. Further research could be conducted to identify the current training programs being offered jointly through the court system and educational institutions, and to determine if these programs reflect findings from this study. Another approach could be to develop action plans and therapeutic programs to prevent domestic violence during acculturation in Nigerian American women.

Moreover, researchers should conduct quantitative studies to empirically validate the findings of this study. For example, researchers could obtain a group of Nigerian women in their native country and a group of Nigerian American women who have transitioned to the United States. Based on this research, they could posit the question *What is the difference in abusive relationships between Nigerian women who have transitioned to the United States and those who have not?* The dependent variable could be degree of abusive relationship that could be measured by an abusive-relationship questionnaire. The independent variable could be type of Nigerian women (have not transitioned, transitioned). These findings could provide important information about whether transitioning to the United States exacerbates the abusive relationships already present in the Nigerian culture.

Existing programs need to implement training of transitional women from Nigeria who have acculturation issues. These women will need resources and therapists to teach them how to survive in America.

Recommendations for Practice

Counselors in the Nigerian American community should consider providing comprehensive and systematic training during the transition process to help ameliorate the stress associated with the cultural change in moving from Nigeria to the United States.

Pretransition training could also be established to help families develop healthier relationships within their new environment.

Limitations

Several limitations existed in this study, including the following: (1) The number of interviewees was small; (2) the length of interviews was limited, (2) only women in Southern California were able to be interviewed, also data only included 20 women, and (4) thematic analysis was limited to the opinions of the researcher, so bias may have been unknowingly introduced. These limitations were mitigated, however, by the fact that participants were given complete anonymity and the researcher followed strict procedural protocol to remain nonjudgmental and unbiased throughout the data-collection process.

Summary

This study investigated how Nigerian women living in Southern California felt about the role of culture and employment conditions on domestic violence in the Nigerian community. Findings provided support that Nigerian women who had transitioned to the United States did not seek assistance for their abuse because they accepted cultural differences and employment conditions as a basis of that abuse. Specifically, the women interviewed felt that their culture drove males to dominate females and gave males final authority in the home. Because of this cultural view, women were portrayed as rebellious if they disobeyed their husbands and the culture subsequently provided neither recourse nor options for the women to find resolution to family problems.

The Nigerian American women interviewed generally felt that moving to the United States was a very emotional event and that problems resulting from the emotional challenge included abuse, anger, fear, lack of support, stress, and financial problems. These women also expressed that their fear to communicate their feelings to their husbands was perhaps the most relevant factor affecting their choice to not seek help and services. Universally, they felt that acculturation contributed to the challenges in their home, and more than half of the respondents attributed fear of retaliation as the reason why they did not seek help.

Findings from the study suggest that the transition from Nigeria to America may exacerbate the instantiated cultural issues and therefore cause women who have moved from Nigeria to America to become even more isolated and afraid than they were before transitioning. Revelations from the study provide a rather grim reality for these families that may take generations to overcome.

REFERENCES

Abasiubong, F., Abasiattai, A. M., Bassey, E. A., & Ogunsemi, O. O. (2010). Demographic risk factors in domestic violence among pregnant women in Uyo, a community in the Niger Delta region, Nigeria. *Health Care for Women International,* 31(10), 891–901. doi:10.1080/07399332.2010.486882

Abraham, U. (2000). "Male order" brides: Immigrant women, domestic violence and immigration law. *Hypatia,* 10(1), 104–119.

Agnew, V. (1998). *In search of a place: Abused women and cultural sensitive service.* Toronto, Canada: University of Toronto Press.

Alhabib, S., Nur, U., & Jones, R. (2010). Domestic violence against women: Systematic review of prevalence studies. *Journal of Family Violence,* 25(4), 369–382.

Anitha, S. (2008). Neither safety nor justice: The UK government response to domestic violence against immigrant women. *Journal of Social Welfare & Family Law,* 30(3), 189–202. doi:10.1080/09649060802550592

Barnish, M. (2004). *Domestic violence: A literature review: Summary.* HM Inspectorate of Probation.

Bartels, L. (2011). Domestic violence: A research agenda.

Beeman, S. (2002). *Evaluating violence against women research reports.* Harrisburg, PA: VAWnet, a project of the National Resource Center on Domestic Violence/Pennsylvania Coalition against Domestic Violence.

Berry, J. W., & Kim, U. (1988). Acculturation and mental health.

Bonomi, A. E., Anderson, M. L., Reid, R. J., Rivara, F. P., Carrell, D., & Thompson, R. S. (2009). Medical and psychosocial diagnoses in women with a history of intimate partner violence. *Archives of Internal Medicine,* 169(18), 1692–1697.

Breitenbecher, R., & Scarce, N. (1999). The association between the perceptions of threat in a dating situation and sexual victimization. *Violence and Victims,* 14(2), 135–146.

Brownridge, D. A. (2002). Cultural variation in male partner violence against women: A comparison of Quebec with the rest of Canada. *Violence against Women,* 8(1), 87–115.

Brush, C. G. (2002). A gendered perspective on organizational creation. *Entrepreneurship Theory and Practice.*

Bui, H. H. (2003, August). A general model for online probabilistic plan recognition. *IJCAI,* 3, 1309–1315.

Campbell, J. C. (2002). Health consequences of intimate partner violence. *The Lancet,* 359(9314), 1331–1336.

Carlson, B. E. (1984). Causes and maintenance of domestic violence: An ecological analysis. *The Social Service Review, 569–587.*

Cohen, S., & Hoberman, H. M. (1983). Positive events and social supports as buffers of life change stress. *Journal of Applied Social Psychology*, 13(2), 99–125.

Coid, J., Petruckevitch, A., Chung, W. S., Richardson, J., Moorey, S., and Feder, G. (2003). Abusive experiences and psychiatric morbidity in women primary care attenders. *The British Journal of Psychiatry*, 183(4), 332–339.

Constable, P. (2012, February 8). *For battered immigrant women, fear of deportation becomes abuser's weapon*. The Washington Post. Retrieved from www.ashingtonpost.org

Constantino, R., Kim, Y., & Crane, P. A. (2005). Effects of a social support intervention on health outcomes in residents of a domestic violence shelter: A pilot study. *Issues in Mental Health Nursing*, 26(6), 575–590.

Constantino, R., Sekula, L. K., Rabin, B., & Stone, C. (2000). Negative life experiences, depression, and immune function in abused and nonabused women. *Biological research for nursing*, 1(3), 190–198.

Coulter, M., & VandeWeerd, C. (2009). Reducing domestic violence and other criminal recidivism: Effectiveness of a multi- level batterers' intervention program. *Violence and Victims*, 24(2), 139–152.

Cousineau, M., & Rondeau, G. (2004). Toward a transnational and cross-culture analysis of family violence: Issue and recommendations. *Violence against Women*, 10(8), 935–949.

Crandall, M. L., Nathens, A. B., & Rivara, F. P. (2004). Injury patterns among female trauma patients: Recognizing intentional injury. *Journal of Trauma-Injury, Infection, and Critical Care*, 57(1), 42–45.

Crowne, S., Juon, H., Ensminger, M., Burrell, L., McFarlane, E., & Duggan, A. (2011). Concurrent and long-term impact of intimate partner violence on employment stability. *Journal of Interpersonal Violence*, 26(6), 1282–1304.

Danziger, S. K., Kalil, A., & Anderson, N. J. (2000). Human capital, physical health, and mental health of welfare recipients: Co-occurrence and correlates. *Journal of Social Issues*, 56(4), 635–654.

Darvishpour, M. (2002). Immigrant women challenge the role of men: How the changing power relationship within Iranian families in Sweden intensifies family conflicts after immigration. *Journal of Comparative Family Studies*, 271–296.

Dasgupta, U. (1998). "Male order" brides: Immigrant women, domestic violence and immigration law. *Hypatia*, 10(1), 104–119.

Davies, M., & Mouzos, J. (2007). *Homicide in Australia: 2005–06 national homicide monitoring program annual report.* Canberra: Australian Institute of Criminology.

Dobash, R., & Dobash, R. (1983). *Violence against wives: A case against patriarchy.* New York: Macmillan Press.

Drachman, D., & Halberstadt, A. (1992). A stage of migration framework as applied to recent Soviet émigrés. *Journal of Multicultural Social Work*, 2(1), 63–78.

Dutton, M., Orloff, L., & Aguilar Hass, G. (2000). Characteristics of help-seeking behaviors, resources, and services needs of battered immigrant Latinas: Legal and policy implications. *Georgetown Journal on Poverty, Law, and Policy*, 7(2).

Edleson, J. L. (2001). Studying the co-occurrence of child maltreatment and domestic violence in families.

Ellsberg, M. (2006). Violence against women and the Millennium Development Goals: Facilitating women's access to support. *International Journal of Gynecology & Obstetrics*, 94(3), 325–332.

Erez, E. (2000). Immigration, culture conflict and domestic violence/ woman battering. *Crime Prevention and Community Safety: An International Journal*, 2(1), 27–36.

Fergusson, D. M., Horwood, L. J., & Ridder, E. M. (2005). Tests of causal linkages between cannabis use and psychotic symptoms. *Addiction*, 100(3), 354–366.

Fisher, E. (2011). Perpetrators of domestic violence: Coordinating responses to complex needs. *Irish Probation Journal*, 8, 124–141.

Friedman, A. R. (1992). Rape and domestic violence: The experience of refugee women. *Women & Therapy*, 13(1–2), 65–78.

Gilchrist, E. A., & Kebbell, M. R. (2010). Intimate partner violence: Current issues in definitions and interventions with perpetrators in the UK. *Forensic Psychology: Concepts, Debates and Practice*, 351–377.

Gondolf, E. W. (2012). *The future of batterer programs: Reassessing evidence-based* practice. UPNE. Retrieved from http://web.ebscohost.com.libproxy.edmc.edu/ehost/details

Graham-Kevan, N. (2007). *Power and control in relationship aggression. Family Interventions in Domestic Violence.* New York: Springer.

Hague, G., & Mullender, A. (2006). Who listens? The voices of domestic violence survivors in service provision in the United Kingdom. *Violence against Women*, 12(6), 568–587.

Hamilton, L., Koehler, J., & Losel, F. (2012). Domestic violence perpetrator programs in Europe, part 1: A survey of current practice. *International Journal of Offender Therapy and Comparative Criminology*. doi:10.1177/0306624X12469506

Hardy, L. J., Getrich, C. M., Quezada, J. C., Guay, A., Michalowski, R. J., & Henley, E. (2012). A call for further research on the impact of state-level immigration policies on public health. *American Journal of Public Health*, 102(7), 1250–1254. doi:10.2105/AJPH.2011.300541

Harwin, N. (2006). Putting a stop to domestic violence in the United Kingdom: Challenges and opportunities. *Violence against Women*, 12(6), 556–567.

Hester, M. (2006). Making it through the criminal justice system: Attrition and domestic violence. *Social Policy and Society*, 5(1), 79–90.

Hindin, M. J., & Adair, L. S. (2002). Who's at risk? Factors associated with intimate partner violence in the Philippines. *Social Science & Medicine*, 55(8), 1385–1399.

Howard, L., Trevillion, K., & Agnew-Davies, R. (2010). Domestic violence and mental health. *International Review of Psychiatry*, 22(5), 525–534.

Hughes, H. M. (1988). Psychological and behavioral correlates of family violence in child witnesses and victims. *American Journal of Orthopsychiatry*, 58(1), 77.

Isiugo-Abanihe, U. C. (2003). *Male role and responsibility in fertility and reproductive health in Nigeria*. Lagos: Ababa Press.

Isiugo-Abanihe, U. C., & Oyedrian, K. A. (2003*). The perceptions of Nigerian women on domestic violence: Evidence from 2003 Nigerian demographic and health survey.* Unpublished manuscript, University of Ibadan, Nigeria.

Kernic, M. A., Wolf, M. E., & Holt, V. L. (2000). Rates and relative risk of hospital admission among women in violent intimate partner relationships. *American Journal of Public Health,* 90(9), 1416.

Kishor, S., & Johnson, K. (2005). Reproductive health and domestic violence: Are the poorest women uniquely disadvantaged? *Demography,* 43(2), 293–307.

Kovacs, K., & Tomison, A. (2003). An analysis of current Australian program initiatives for children exposed to domestic violence. *Australian Journal of Social Issues,* 38(4), 513.

Ladepo, A. (2014, January 22). An Epidemic: Nigerian men killing their nurse wives in the US. Sahara Reporters.

Laing, L. (2003). *Routine screening for domestic violence.* Topic Paper, Australian Domestic and Family Violence Clearinghouse, University of New South Wales, Sydney, Australia.

Lewchuk, W., de Wolff, A., King, A., & Polanyi, M. (2003). From job strain to employment strain: Health effects of precarious employment. *Just Labour,* 3(Fall), 23–35.

Liao, M. (2006). Domestic violence among Asian Indian immigrant women: Risk factors, acculturation, and intervention. *Women & Therapy,* 29(1/2), 23–39.

Lichter, E. L., & McCloskey, L. A. (2004). The effects of childhood exposure to marital violence on adolescent gender role beliefs and dating violence. *Psychology of Women Quarterly*, 28(4), 344–357.

Liebmann, T. (2012). Ethical advocacy for immigrant survivors of family crisis. *Family Court Review*, 50(4), 650–661. doi:10.111 1/j.1744–1617.2012.01483

Litrownik, A. J., Newton, R., Hunter, W. M., English, D., & Everson, M. D. (2003). Exposure to family violence in young at- risk children: A longitudinal look at the effects of victimization and witnessed physical and psychological aggression. *Journal of Family Violence*, 18(1), 59–73.

Madoc-Jones, I., & Roscoe, K. (2010). Women's safety service within the Integrated Domestic Abuse Programme: Perceptions of service users. *Child and Family Social Work*, 15(2), 155–164. doi:10.1111/j.1365–2206.2009.00647.x

Mann, J., & Takyi, B. (2009). Autonomy, dependence or culture: Examining the impact of resources and socio-cultural processes on attitudes towards intimate partner violence in Ghana, Africa. *Journal of Family Violence*, 24(5), 323–335. doi:10.1007/ s10896-009-9232-9

Martin, S., Moracco, K., Garro, J., Tsui, A., Kupper, L., Chase, J., & Campbell, J. (2002). Domestic violence across generations: Findings from northern India. *International Journal of Epidemiology*, 31(3), 560–572.

Mayer, B. W., & Coulter, M. (2002). Psychosocial aspects of partner abuse. *American Journal of Nursing*, 102(6), 24AA–24CC.

McBride, A. B., & Campbell, S. (1998). Feminist research methodology. In Encyclopedia of Nursing Research (pp. 199–201). New York: Springer.

Mcmurran, M., & Gilchrist, E. (2008). Anger control and alcohol use: Appropriate interventions for perpetrators of domestic violence? *Psychology, Crime & Law*, 14(2), 107–116.

Meisel, J., Chandler, D., & Rienzi, B. M. (2003). Domestic violence prevalence and effects on employment in two California TANF populations. *Violence against Women*, 9(10), 1191–1212.

Moe, A. M., & Bell, M. P. (2004). Abject economics: The effects of battering and violence on women's work and employability. *Violence against Women*, 10(1), 29–55.

Moffitt, T. E., Caspi, A., & Rutter, M. (2005). Strategy for investigating interactions between measured genes and measured environments. *Archives of General Psychiatry*, 62(5), 473–481.

Moylan, C. A., Herrenkohl, T. I., Sousa, C., Tajima, E. A., Herrenkohl, R. C., & Russo, M. J. (2009). Effects of child abuse and exposure to domestic violence on adolescent internalizing and externalizing behavior problems. *Journal of Family Violence*, 25(1), 53–63. doi:10.1007/s10896-009-9269-9

Mullender, A., & Burton, S. (2001). Dealing with perpetrators. What Works in Reducing Domestic Violence: A comprehensive guide for professionals. London, England: Whiting and Birch.

Narayan, U. (1995). "Male order" brides: Immigrant women, domestic violence and immigration law. *Hypatia*, 10(1), 104–119.

Nasir, K., & Hyder, A. A. (2003). Violence against pregnant women in developing countries: Review of evidence. *European Journal of Public Health, 13*(2), 105–107.

Neggers, Y., Goldenberg, R., Cliver, S., & Hauth, J. (2004). Effects of domestic violence on preterm birth and low birth weight. *Acta obstetricia et gynecologica Scandinavica, 83*(5), 455–460.

Nelson, H. D., Nygren, P., McInerney, Y., & Klein, J. (2004). Screening women and elderly adults for family and intimate partner violence: A review of the evidence for the US Preventive Services Task Force. *Annals of Internal Medicine, 140*(5), 387–396.

Nigeria Demographic and Health Survey 2003. (2003). Retrieved from http://dhsprogram.com/pubs/pdf/FR148/FR148.pdf

Nilsson, J., Brown, C., Russell, E., & Khamphakdy-Brown, S. (2008). Acculturation, partner violence, and psychological distress in refugee women from Somalia. *Journal of Interpersonal Violence, 23*(11), 1654–1663.

Nwokocha, E. E. (2004). Gender inequality and contradictions in West African development: The need for centriarchy. *African Journal for the Psychological Study of Social Issues, 7*(1), 30–47.

Nworah, U. (2010). *Violence against women in the Nigerian community: Issues of power and control.*

Obi, S. N., & Ozumba, B. C. (2007). Factors associated with domestic violence in southeast Nigeria. *Journal of Obstetrics and Gynaecology, 27*(1), 75–78.

Odimegwu, C. O. (2001, July). Couple formation and domestic violence among the Tiv of Benue State, Nigeria. In *International Colloquium, Gender Popul. Dev. Afr. Abidjan* (pp. 16–21).

O'Leary, P., Chung, D., & Zannettino, L. (2004). A comparative assessment of good practice in programs for men who use violence against female partners.

Oropesa, R. S. (1997). Development and marital power in Mexico. *Social Forces*, 75(4), 1291–1318.

Plichta, S. B. (2007). Interactions between victims of intimate partner violence against women and the health care system policy and practice implications. *Trauma, Violence, & Abuse*, 8(2), 226–239.

Porter, M., & Haslam, N. (2005). Predisplacement and postdisplacement factors associated with mental health of refugees and internally displaced persons: A meta-analysis. *JAMA*, 294(5), 602–612.

Reeves, C., & O'Leary-Kelly, A. M. (2007). The effects and costs of intimate partner violence for work organizations. *Journal of Interpersonal Violence*, 22(3), 327–344.

Rennison, C., & Planty, M. (2003). Nonlethal intimate partner violence: Examining race, gender, and income patterns. Violence and Victims, 18(4), 433–443.

Rianon, N. J., & Shelton, A. J. (2003). Perception of spousal abuse expressed by married Bangladeshi immigrant women in Houston, Texas, USA. *Journal of Immigrant Health*, 5(1), 37–44.

Richards, K. (2011). Children's exposure to domestic violence in Australia. *Trends & Issues in Crime and Criminal Justice*, 419,1.

Riger, S., Staggs, S. L., & Schewe, P. (2004). Intimate partner violence as an obstacle to employment among mothers affected by welfare reform. *Journal of Social Issues*, 60(4), 801–818.

Romero, D., Chavkin, W., Wise, P. H., & Smith, L. A. (2003). Low-income mothers' experience with poor health, hardship, work, and violence implications for policy. *Violence against Women, 9*(10), 1231–1244.

Staggs, S. L., & Riger, S. (2005). Effects of intimate partner violence on low-income women's health and employment. *American Journal of Community Psychology, 36*(1–2), 133–145.

Statistics Canada. (2002). *Census Standard data products Statistics Canada 2001.* Retrieved from http://www12.stacan.ca/English/censusol/products /standard/themes/retrieve

Straus, M. (1999). The controversy over domestic violence by women. *Violence in Intimate Relationships,* 17–44.

Suermann, H. (1997). Timothy and his concern for the School of Basos. *The Harp, 10*(1–2), 51–58.

Sullivan, M., Senturia, K., Negash, T., Shiu-Thornton, S., & Giday, B. (2005). "For us it is like living in the dark": Ethiopian women's experiences with domestic violence. *Journal of Interpersonal Violence, 20*(8), 922–940.

Swanberg, J. E., & Logan, T. K. (2005). Domestic violence and employment: A qualitative study. *Journal of Occupational Health Psychology, 10*(1), 3.

Swanberg, J. E., Macke, C., & Logan, T. K. (2006). Intimate partner violence, women, and work: Coping on the job. *Violence and Victims, 21*(5), 561–578.

Tajima, E. A. (2004). Correlates of the co-occurrence of wife abuse and child abuse among a representative sample. *Journal of Family Violence, 19*(6), 391–402.

Taylor, J., Cheers, B., Weetra, C., & Gentle, I. (2004). Supporting community solutions to family violence. *Australian Social Work,* 57(1), 71–83.

Thurston, W. E., & Eisener, A. C. (2006). Successful integration and maintenance of screening for domestic violence in the health sector moving beyond individual responsibility. *Trauma, Violence, and Abuse,* 7(2), 83–92.

Tilden, V. P., Schmidt, T., Limandri, B. J., Chiodo, G. T., Garland, M. J., & Loveless, P. A. (1994). Factors that influence clinicians' assessment and management of family violence. *American Journal of Public Health,* 84(4), 628–633.

Tjaden, P., & Thoennes, N. (2000). Prevalence and consequences of male-to-female and female-to-male intimate partner violence as measured by the National Violence against Women Survey. *Violence against Women,* 6(2), 142–161.Tolman, R. M.,

& Rosen, D. (2001). Domestic violence in the lives of women receiving welfare mental health, substance dependence, and economic well-being. *Violence against Women,* 7(2), 141–158.

Umoh, A. V., Abah, G. M., Ugege, W. E., & Inyangetoh, E. C. (2012). Prevalence and attitude of women to spousal physical abuse in pregnancy in a Niger Delta community of Nigeria. *TAF Preventive Medicine Bulletin,* 11(6), 731–736.

Vogel, L., & Marshall, L. L. (2001). PTSD symptoms and partner abuse: Low income women at risk. *Journal of Traumatic Stress,* 14(3), 569–584.

Walker, L. (1984). The battered woman, 1979. *The Battered Woman Syndrome.*

Wathen, C. N., &and MacMillan, H. L. (2003). Interventions for violence against women: Scientific review. *JAMA*, 289(5), 589–600.

Westwood, M. J., & Ishiyama, F. (1991). Challenges in counseling immigrant clients: Understanding intercultural barriers to career adjustment. *Journal of Employment Counseling*, 28(4), 130–143.

Winkelman, M. (1994). Cultural shock and adaptation. *Journal of Counseling & Development*, 73(2), 121–126.

Wisner, C. L., Gilmer, T. P., Saltzman, L. E., & Zink, T. M. (1999). Intimate partner violence against women: Do victims cost health plans more? *Journal of Family Practice*, 48(6), 439–443.

Woodtli, M. A. (2000). Domestic violence and the nursing curriculum: Tuning in and tuning up. *Journal of Nursing Education*, 39(4), 173–182.

World Health Organization (WHO). (1999). *Ethical and safety recommendations for research on domestic violence against women.* Department of Gender and Women's Health Family and Community Health. Retrieved from http://www.who.int/gender/documents/vawethics/en/

Yearnshire, S. (1997). Analysis of cohort. *Violence against Women. London: Royal College of Obstetricians and Gynaecologists (RCOG).*

APPENDICES

APPENDICES

APPENDIX A

Interview Questions

1. What is your age range?
   a. 18–25
   b. 25–35
   c. 35–45
   d. 45 and over
2. Are you
   abuse victim?
   abuse survivor?
   friend or family of abuse victim?
   friend or family of abuser?
3. Does male-dominated culture contribute to domestic abuse? (Yes or No)
4. Does fear of being deported stop women who are being abused from seeking help for domestic abuse? (Yes or No)
5. Does fear of financial issues contribute to not seeking help for domestic abuse? (Yes or No)
6. Does higher education or professional employment stop abused women from seeking help? (Yes or No)
7. What is your view of society when it comes to seeking help for domestic abuse?
   a. Good
   b. Fair

    c.   Poor

    d.   None of the above

8.   Do you think the Nigerian community accepts domestic abuse due to cultural beliefs and practices? (Yes or No)

9.   Does alcohol abuse contribute to domestic abuse? (Yes or No)

10. Does unemployment contribute to domestic abuse? (Yes or No)

Printed in the United States
by Baker & Taylor Publisher Services